T0063343

Dedicated to the Glory of God and to the
magnificent family He gave me.

To my husband Bucky, the wheels of your love will turn
my world forever. I'll love you now and for all time.

To my children, Kyle, Kari, Johnathan, William
and those yet to come. You are the sweetest
treasure of my life. You hold my heart forever.

To my dearest family and friends, God fills my time on
this earth with the most precious people on the planet.

CONTENTS

I dashed into the busy Chicago airport, sprinted to the ticket counter then raced to join hundreds of Monday morning travelers moving rapidly through the security line. My full-speed-ahead mode left me temporarily ahead of schedule and gave me a little time for one of my favorite pastimes: people watching. The scene resembled the chaos that ensues when directing the full force of a water hose on an ant bed. Thousands of frantic creatures scrambled around, although it was difficult to determine exactly where they were headed.

The flight information boards were flashing times... departures... arrivals... delays. I suddenly found myself swept up in the anguish, stress, and madness of a multitude of people I didn't even know. But even though I didn't know their names – I could feel the knots of anxiety twisting in their stomachs. I felt their rising tension as they reached the closing doors only to watch the train to Concourse D leave without them.

I know what it's like to exert all your effort to meet life's deadlines only to miss them by a fraction of a second. I know how it feels to be worn out from the race when you are nowhere near the finish line. I know the overwhelming despair of realizing you will never reach the goal line. And yes, I have also sung the popular refrain, "There are not enough hours in the day."

But on that crazy Monday morning, God whispered sweet hope to me, and reminded me that His word offers answers to all of life's dilemmas – even my time management problems!

To all the tired, frantic, and overwhelmed, God offers us the peace that's found in trusting His Perfect Timing. It's my prayer that you will find in the pages of this little book, lessons on how to enjoy your time and how to use it wisely.

Yours Truly,

Kathy Walters Burnsed –

the former reigning Queen of Frantic.

Teach us to use wisely, all the time we have.

Psalms 90:12 CEV

TIME OUT!

The other day in the middle of the hectic horror of life in the fast lane, I cleared my throat, and with all the projection technique I could remember from my freshman college drama class, complete with the hand motions, I declared, "TIME OUT!" I'd heard this phrase used at national sporting events, at the local, little league football game, and by my kindergarten teacher. I'd seen the response it rendered and felt confident that my convincing performance would freeze-frame time.

I dreamed of stopping the clock, for a few minutes at least, and figured that five or ten minutes of stillness would give me the competitive edge I needed to rule the world. Or at least, manage, my world. The excitement began to mount as I contemplated the possibilities of controlling my time. And then my husband shook me awake. "Honey, get up! We overslept! We're late! We're going to miss our flight!"

And so it goes. Time marches on, but how can I keep time from marching over me? How can I beat the clock? I wonder if that new, deluxe executive three-year day planner that links directly to my smart phone will help. Maybe I need to attend another time management seminar. Or maybe, I should just forget it all and give up already! In reality, I have no time to devote to learning how to link the executive, three-year day planner to my smart phone; no time to squeeze in another time management seminar, and even giving up would cause a backlog on the To Do List.

This was my recurring dilemma. And each time I thought I'd found a way to organize my world and align my time with the demands of the day, there was another plane I'd miss; another To Do List crumpled and tossed into the trash can. What a failure! I felt like Tony and Maria in *Westside Story,* vainly holding on to the hope that they would find time.

> *There's a time for us*
> *Somewhere a place for us.*
> *Peace and quiet and open air.*
> *Wait for us, somewhere.*
> *There's a time for us,*
> *Someday a time for us,*
> *Time together with time to spare,*
> *Time to look, time to care,*
> *Someday! Somehow, Somewhere!*

Although it sounded wonderful, at the same time I realized that Tony and Maria's story ended rather tragically. Time, for them, came to a screeching halt. So, where do we go from here?

Lesson Number One: instead of trying to **manage time** we must learn to **value time!**

While it's inconvenient to be out of gas, out of luck or out of money, being out of time is far more serious. Wasting your resources isn't smart, but wasting your time is much worse.

Your luck can change and money can be regained, but one thing we can't recycle or reclaim is time. We either use it – or lose it! Have you ever reached the end of the day and wondered what you'd accomplished? I have. It made me wonder how other people spent their time. Look what I found on a recent survey from a U.S. News and World Report. The average American spends:

- Six months sitting at stoplights (I am confident the average is higher in my city)
- Eight months opening junk mail (This probably only includes Postal Service mail)
- One year looking for misplaced things (What's the remote doing in the fridge?)
- Two years unsuccessfully returning phone calls. (Tag, you're it!)
- Four years doing housework (even if you never bother to dust!)
- Five years of waiting in line (an area in which I score above average!)
- Six years eating (look around to determine who's logged more dining hours)

While we can't control stoplights, waiting in line, or the need to eat, we can decide how to spend our time pursuing those things in life that matter most to us. In fact, someone once said, "Show me how you spend your time, and I will show you what's important to you." Each moment we have is precious and time is truly our most valuable resource.

We create elaborate financial plans, but what about setting aside time to plan how to use the twenty four hours God has given us each day? If we don't plan our time, somebody else surely will. A great place to start this process is to look at your schedule. Where do you invest the most time? An honest analysis may be shocking. Facing the facts is always a great place to begin as you reach for the best return on your time investment.

Take the time to examine your time!

Look carefully then how you walk, not as unwise but as wise, making the best use of the time, because the days are evil. Therefore do not be foolish, but understand what the will of the Lord is.

Ephesians 5:15-17 ESV

The Process of Time

The pursuit and study of a good time management plan began on that crazy, manic Monday at the O'Hare Airport. I couldn't shake the frantic and panicked look on the faces of those desperately trying to beat the clock. Their pain was all too familiar. How could we win this war?

I needed to find a way to manage time. The best way to ensure optimum performance on a product is to go to the manufacturer's handbook. Our search begins, and Genesis is the best place to start.

And in the *process of time* it came to pass (Genesis 4:3)

Now in the *process of time* (Genesis 38:12)

It happened in the *process of time* (Exodus 2:23)

It came to pass in the *process of time* (Judges 11:4)

2 Chronicles 21:19 (I tried not to laugh). "And it came to pass, that in the *process of time*, after the end of two years, Libnah's bowels fell out by reason of his sickness: so he died of sore diseases." (KJV) Oh, good Grief! The *process* can really get messy, and besides, I'm not a process kind of girl. Seriously, if I can't lose 82 pounds or write a comprehensive book on Time Management by next Tuesday, I am not interested. The aversion to the process of time made my life difficult and nearly impossible.

My Bible study was "grab and go." Read a Psalm; throw in a Proverb. This lack of *process* made for a shallow little church girl who was just checking off all the boxes. I put off (a south Georgia term for procrastinated) going on a sensible diet, starting an exercise program, writing that book, even saving for a dream vacation because those things involved a process and couldn't be accomplished in a day.

Fortunately, God, the creator of time, patiently waited and constantly called me to trade the crown I received as the reigning "Queen of Frantic" for the peace found in His perfect timing. Trust me, this has been a process!

Perhaps all of this explains my To Do list addiction. Don't get me wrong, the To Do list is a great tool we will discuss in a later chapter, but my obsession wasn't the answer to good time management. I love a plan. I would often find myself at the end of a day admiring my accomplishments. If I had completed any unexpected tasks, I would add them to the list, just to have the sheer pleasure of checking them off. The check, often in a red marker for effect, meant completed, done, efficiently, and quickly.

A long list and a busy schedule with lots of red marks must mean I was an excellent time manager. Right? God must be smiling on my frantic activity.

My mad dash to gather all the "time" scriptures (well over 600, if anybody is counting) left me in an interesting predicament. I had always hurried through my bible study gleaning a few "feel good" verses, while I watched my precious friends pore over the word of God. They would glean golden nuggets and deep spiritual truths. How could I ever realize God's time management plan if I was racing through the list of scriptures?

For me, checking off the boxes was what it was all about. But God was really more interested in teaching me about the process of time.

What is the process of time? What does that mean? According to one business dictionary, *The Process of Time* is defined as the period when one or more inputs are transformed into a finished product. That seems a little understated to me! Obviously, the person writing that left out the emotion, the chaos, and the stress of the interruptions.

I found it interesting that the definition for the process of time in the business dictionary also mentioned, "A business will typically seek to minimize its process time for a particular manufactured good without compromising quality to the point where consumers would purchase less of it."

While spending so much time trying to minimize the time we spend in *the process*, quality of time is compromised. We are so busy trying to accelerate into the future, longing to realize the finished product. We must learn to value the precious and sometimes not so precious time we spend during the process. This is a place of learning, growing and maturing so we will be equipped to handle the finished product.

If you have ever learned or taught a kid to ride a bike, then you will understand this principle. Let's say the process begins with a "Kid's Ride On". No pedals. Close to the ground. Then comes the graduation to the Big Wheel. Lots of muscle power is required to power this toddler favorite, but eventually the kid outgrows it. Next, the shiny red tricycle arrives. This makes it easier to travel a longer distance and even uphill. Great memories are made, photo opportunities, and then it's time for the bike with training wheels for balance.

In the process of time, each step gives you training, confidence and the balance to graduate to the two-wheeler. No loving, caring parent would allow you to skip to the ten-speed. Likewise, God allows us the process of time to teach us and to spare us from the dreadful outcome of flesh on the pavement on our first spin around the block.

Lesson Number Two: Remember the lessons you learn *in the process*. They are invaluable!

But when the fullness of time had come, God sent forth his Son, born of woman, born under the law, to redeem those who were under the law, so that we might receive adoption as sons. And because you are sons, God has sent the Spirit of his Son into our hearts, crying, "Abba! Father!" So you are no longer a slave, but a son, and if a son, then an heir of God through Christ.

Galatians 4:4-7 NKJ

And Suddenly

The process of time is often followed by "and suddenly!" Let me put that in more relatable terms. Out of the blue, unexpectedly and sometimes downright alarming!

Imagine a dark starry night in a field on the edge of town, and you run into a band of ragtag sheep attendants. The job isn't glamorous. The pay is pathetic. Co-workers are on each other's nerves and there is no paid leave and no time off. Dreams have faded and hope for a better day is gone.

And suddenly, there was with the angel a multitude of the heavenly host praising God and saying *"Glory to God in the highest, and on earth peace, good will toward men."* The long awaited Savior had just entered a world that had lost all hope in the process of time. The Messiah came to a weary people whose dream of redemption or better times had faded.

Then, suddenly in the sky, and out of the blue, an angel choir delivers an unexpected proclamation of good news. Seriously, we know face-to-face encounters with angels tend to be alarming. Please take note that angels rarely use the "Hello" or "Good evening" salutation. Their typical opening line is "Fear not!" So yes, it was alarming.

Perhaps, the abruptness of an -*and suddenly* moment- is what makes us jump. After praying, longing, waiting and giving up, we tend to wonder exactly what is happening. Often, it doesn't come in the form we were expecting. We are expecting a regal king and a baby in a manger shows up instead. God's Plan. God's Timing.

Let's explore the *suddenly* notion a little more. Yes, it seemed *suddenly*, but only because the shepherds weren't privy to the plan. God was setting everything in place. In Galatians 4:4-7 we learn it was all about timing.

> *But when the fullness of time had come, God sent*
> *forth his Son, born of woman, born under the law,*

*to redeem those who were under the law, so that
we might receive adoption as sons. And because you
are sons, God has sent the Spirit of his Son into our
hearts, crying, "Abba! Father!" So you are no longer
a slave, but a son, and if a son, then an heir of God
through Christ.*

The Redeemer came right on time. Right on schedule. And although it seemed a long time in coming, it happened when each piece of the puzzle was perfectly laid in place.

Perhaps you have experienced another kind of *and suddenly* moment. This event is not accompanied by angels singing and great rejoicing. Everything seems to be going along at a happy pace *and suddenly* you are notified of a layoff, your lab results are abnormal or your long term relationship ends. You are caught by surprise. The timing seems all wrong and you wonder if things will ever get back in sync.

Are you familiar with Joseph of Genesis (the first book of the Bible not the British rock band)? Joseph was the guy with the amazing Technicolor dream coat.

Genesis 37:3-4 makes it clear; he was his father's favorite.

Now Israel (Jacob) loved Joseph more than all his children, because he was the son of his old age. Also he made him a tunic of many colors. But when his brothers saw that their father loved him more than all his brothers, they hated him and could not speak peaceably to him.

Joseph, as a seventeen year old, had all the perks and privileges of a spoiled rich kid. His father spared no expense and lavished him with at least one (no doubt more) extravagant gift. We can credit timing for this! Jacob's gush of affection was a result of the timing of Joseph's birth –because he was the son of his old age. Let's just call this the Grandparent Syndrome. Can anybody relate? Folks, who at one time, possessed great parenting skills, restraint, strict standards and discipline lose it when the grandkids show up! Ice Cream before dinner? Sure! Shopping spree at Toys-R-Us? Absolutely!

Joseph's early life was a dream. He exuded confidence and knew his future included a position of prominence. However, his boastful boyish babbling got him in trouble. *Genesis 37:5*

Now Joseph had a dream, and he told it to his brothers; and they hated him even more. It was at this point that *suddenly*, things took a dramatic downward turn (in a pit) for Joseph. His brothers contemplated murder. But, at the insistence of his older brother Reuben, opted to get rid of him by selling him into slavery. Talk about bad timing... all of this right before his Senior Prom!

Fortunately, the story doesn't end here. Your story may contain a series of suddenly(s) that make you feel like you are swirling down the drain. Don't lose hope. Your dream is not dead, just delayed. Hang on, the ride could contain more twists, turns and sudden drops than Disney's Space Mountain. As, in the case of the thrill ride roller coaster, it usually all happens in the dark. Since you can't see what is ahead, you should just hold on tight and trust that whoever designed this course knew what they were doing.

Joseph's ride took him to Egypt where he prospered. The scripture says that the Lord made everything he put his hand to prosper. He was promoted (up) to a position of power. Then, he was falsely accused by the flirtatious wife of his boss, Potiphar. This landed him a new office (down) in the bottom cell block of the Cairo Federal Prison. Not to belabor the issue here, but even when Joseph was serving time, he found favor with the warden and was placed in charge. Please note Joseph had no idea how much time he would have to serve. The fact he had not been put to death for the charges that were leveled against him was miraculous.

There are several things that are striking about how he conducts himself. No record is found of him complaining, whining, or squirming to get out of the situation. Not even any trash talk about brothers who hated him or the deceitful dame that lied about him. Rather, Joseph can be found putting his effort into making his surroundings a prosperous place (whether the palace or the prison).

Genesis 39:22-23 puts it in perspective.

> *And the keeper of the prison committed to Joseph's hand all the prisoners who were in the prison; whatever they did there, it was his doing. The keeper of the prison did not look into anything that was under Joseph's authority, because the LORD was with him; and whatever he did, the LORD made it prosper.*

In her book *Complaint Free Living* (a good short read for us busy folks), life coach and author, Emra Smith, discusses the benefits of committing to eliminating time consuming, erosive, *negative talk*. She issues five life challenges that, when accepted, will result in a joyous and prosperous life. LoveLivingToday.net discusses some of the divine truths and devotion we see in the life and character of Joseph.

In the darkroom of life, we see the character and integrity of Joseph immerging.

It takes time to develop a crisp, clean picture. Joseph waits it out. We don't find him complaining or compromising his character.

Prison wasn't Joseph's final stop. Yet another *and suddenly* moment moves him into the second highest position in the land. One day he is washing pots and pans in the prison chow hall and the next he is Pharaoh's right hand man as ruler over Egypt. My, what a difference a day makes!

So Fear Not! Don't be scared silly by the *and suddenly(s)* of life.

Lesson Number Three: *Suddenly* is often the setup for an incredible season in your life!

To everything there is a season, a time for every

purpose under heaven:

Ecclesiastes 3:1 NKJ

LET'S ASK SOLOMON

You would think that wise old King Solomon could offer us some great time management tips. After all, he was the writer of the familiar prose – there is a time for everything. Imagine how his day planner looked with everything neatly in place. Scripture tells us he took on great projects, including building houses, municipal planning of gardens and parks, farming, owning many flocks and herds, amassing a fortune, managing servants, and dealing with the PMS factor of a thousand women (700 wives and 300 concubines). Okay, so all of his time expenditures were not God honoring! In this chapter, we explore how to honor God with the way we spend our time, and how to skip those things that are not God pleasing. Those things led to the cry of Solomon in Ecclesiastes 2:17, "*So, I hated my life.*"

What? Hated your life? Solomon, come, on! Really? You are the guy that had it all.

Ecclesiastes 2:10 gives us an idea of how Solomon operated.

> "*Whatever my eyes desired I did not keep from them.*
> *I did not withhold my heart from any pleasure, for*
> *my heart rejoiced in all my labor,*" *Ecclesiastes 2:10*

Who has time to do all they need to do, much less, everything they desire?

The man with everything, who busied himself with good things must have skipped the most important elements of spending his time well, and we find him here in a mess and hating life. Many have this same issue today. We spend time trying to find fulfillment, satisfaction and enjoyment and we come up short! Instead we could describe our lives as exhausting, disappointing, frustrating and overwhelming because there doesn't seem to be enough hours in the day!

Thankfully we see Solomon maturing a little in Chapter 3. The older (at least by a chapter) and wiser Solomon finally realizes that schedules that are packed, filled, and even well managed must be submitted to God. He is the only one who can make the timetable work beautifully.

> *Ecclesiastes 3:9-11 What do workers gain from their toil? I have seen the burden God has laid on the human race. He has made everything beautiful in its time. He has also set eternity in the human heart; yet no one can fathom what God has done from beginning to end.*

The picture is clearer when we view our schedules through our heart and not our heads. God has placed in our hearts an eternal lens. We need to view our schedule through the lens of eternity not our 6 o'clock deadline. Much of Solomon's frustration came from knowing (his mind) that all the things he busied himself with would not even be thought of after his death. All of his efforts, blood, sweat and tears would be buried with him. Solomon appears tormented by this notion.

We find Solomon getting a better handle on the situation in I Kings 3:3. There is nothing like a conversation with God to set things in order! In a dream one night God asked Solomon, "What do you want?" Wow, try to answer that one! More money? What about more time!? Solomon nailed it! Lord, I will take wisdom. I Kings 3:9 *Give therefore thy servant an understanding heart.*

We don't have a time management problem. We lack wisdom! See, I thought that I lacked the time to get everything accomplished... what I really lacked was the wisdom.

We need the understanding that enables us to make the right time investments! The good news is we don't have to read between the lines or follow some philosophical trail. In the New Testament, James gives us a simple way to achieve this understanding.

> *James 1:5 If any of you lacks wisdom, let him ask of God, who gives to all liberally and without reproach, and it will be given to him.*

It is pretty simple. We make it difficult when we don't desire or seek those things that God wants to freely give us.

Solomon got this one right! Wisdom. Good answer!

Lesson Number Four: Rather than asking Solomon (or any other good time manager), ask God. He is the only one that can give you the wisdom you need to manage your days!

Walk in wisdom toward those who are outside, redeeming the time. ⁶ Let your speech always be with grace, seasoned with salt, that you may know how you ought to answer each one.

Colossians 4:5–6 NKJ

THE TO DO LIST

Is the To Do list a great time management tool? Yes! Can you check off all the items on your list and still be a lousy time manager? Yes!

This is a very practical component of time management. My approach may be a little unconventional, but it works!

Anybody a list person? Wow, the power of a plan! I like to do a review of my day and draft the list for tomorrow before I go to bed each night. A list motivates me. I get such satisfaction out of a list, I find myself adding any unexpected accomplishments so I can have the moment of sheer pleasure that comes from checking it off.

My To Do List looks like this:

Now *(today)* _____

_____

_____

Next (tomorrow) _____

_____

_____

Not Now (maybe never) _____

_____

_____

I place the things that I must accomplish (in order of priority) in the *Now (today)* category. These are things that if the sun goes down today and they are undone there will be serious consequences. Most folks overload this category with things they would like to get done. Put those things in the *Next (tomorrow)* category. When you have finished the Must-dos, you can move those up. I shoot for 3 items in the *Now* (the Must) list. By concentrating only on those items, I am usually finished with my main objectives early and can move on to the less pressing part of my list.

The *Next* category is exactly that -*Next!* We simply move to this category upon completion of the *Now* Category. The items on the *Next* list things may become a top priority later, but for *Now* they are just **Next** (or tomorrow).

The great thrill of moving tomorrow's items up to today (when time permits) is exhilarating! And then there is the *Not Now* (maybe never) category. These are the things that I am determined to avoid today. Maybe it is some time wasters I have identified or bad habits I am trying to break. *Not Now* is more palatable than *never.* In order to reach my goal, I won't have a double-fudge brownie with ice cream today -*Not Now.* When I reach my weight goal it won't be completely out of the question.

Don't get too wrapped around your list. Sometimes, the schedule dramatically changes from morning to afternoon. For this reason, I prefer to use a pencil for my list. Delete works the same way on electronic devices. The more flexible, available and sensitive we are, the less frustration we will experience.

The beauty of placing only those critical items on the *Now* list is that you *now* have time for interruptions! You might as well have room in your schedule for them. Some days you will have more interruptions than others. Interruptions are inevitable. This system allows space for the unexpected and keeps you on track.

But how should we determine what makes the list? *Now, Next, or Never.* This simple question will help you determine what makes it on the list. <u>Is this activity getting me closer to my goal or is it increasing the distance between me and my goal?</u>

If your number one goal in life is to have meaningful relationships, then everything you do should all go through that filter. Is the time I am going to spend on this project going to help me achieve my goals? If the answer is yes, then go for it! If you aren't sure then pause and examine it. We often give little or no thought to our time expenditures. Often, we don't even stop to whisper a prayer. Lord, I need your wisdom. We must take the time to listen to His instruction.

Lesson Number Five: Prayerfully Prioritize. Now? Next? Not Now? Or Never?

For as many as are led by the Spirit, These are the Sons of God.

Romans 8:19 NKJ

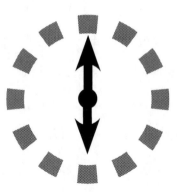

Hearing the Holy Spirit over the Tic-Tock

"I can't hear you," I exclaimed. I was getting ready for the day. The blow dryer was on the high setting. The radio was blaring. I was trying to catch the morning weather report over my hair styling apparatus when the grandfather clock started its hourly ritual… ding, dong!

The collision of these sounds, punctuated by the old clock, reminded me I was running late. It made it impossible to hear the information my husband was trying to share with me from the other room. He wanted to give me his schedule for the day.

This was the morning routine. We scrambled to get the day started. I considered it the start of the spin cycle.

Little did I realize that when you add two precious toddlers to the mix, you have the recipe for mayhem. It is truly miraculous that we made it out of this season of madness alive. Our young family was energetic, enthusiastic, and yes, insane.

My job(s) as fulltime wife, mother and director of a state-of-the-art television production facility required the juggling skills of a veteran circus clown. Trust me, many days I was tempted to run away and join the circus! Oh, did I mention, I was employed by a local ministry as their media director? My fulltime (65-70 hours a week) job was spreading the good news.

Early each day I would drop my precious ones (13 months apart) at the church daycare. Each evening we were the last parents to pick up the children. I was convinced that my activity had God's blessing. After all, I was working for a church. I was in ministry! By the end of the seven year run, I was spent. Each week I could feel myself getting weaker physically, and mentality. And if I was feeling so tired, just imagine how worn out my little ones were? My husband and I worked to keep our family and frantic schedules afloat, but it seemed that our boat was taking on water. I am thankful that God so graciously changed our circumstance before our ship sank! They warn you in lifeguard class that the drowning victim will fight you. I wish I was the exception.

The unnoticed reality (by me and others, I supposed) was that I was spiritually depleted. Not only was I not hearing the voice of the Holy Spirit over the clatter, frankly, I never took any time to listen. How could I manage a hectic schedule without the guidance of the Holy Spirit? I would soon realize that time management has nothing to do with how many items are on your To Do list.

My husband's job moved us to another state. With the largest moving van available, the kids, and two dogs in tow, we said our goodbyes to all we had ever known. Our native home and fast paced, high profile lifestyle were in the rear view mirror. I believed that the still, sleepy town that lay ahead would be the answer to all my time and scheduling issues. How exciting to face the upcoming months without having to report to the office, meet deadlines or cope with a never ending list of social obligations.

Visions of baking cookies, gardening, lazy afternoons at the lake and getting my children situated into K-5 and first grade were filling my head. Finally, my schedule was going to make sense. My fairy tale timetable was coming true. Not!

The unpacking was completed in record time. Pictures were in place and packing boxes were at the recycling center within a week. No time to dilly-dally. I had to begin my regiment of rest!

I was invited by a friend to guest teach a Sunday school class at the local church we would be attending. My first meeting with new people in my new town... exciting! I certainly wanted to pick the right topic. A subject that would wow the crowd and make the class clamor to befriend this recent transplant was in order. I searched through some of my sweetest material. Aha! Elijah by the Brook (I Kings 17) is a great lesson. The well used and worn notes indicated this was a favorite passage of mine.

A quick refresher on the material and I was off to present the proclamation of God's plan and provision for one of His most choice servants, Elijah. I had been over the material a million (slight exaggeration) times. Each time I posed several questions. Have you ever relocated to a new town? Changed schools? Joined a new church? The list of questions struck me as odd. To this point I had only imagined how far out of the comfort zone these situations would find one. My answer sheet for this quiz read no, no and no. Until that moment! This was an interesting turn in that message.

Chapter 17 of 1 Kings introduces Elijah, the prophet as a well known Tishbite in Gilead. He had a place of prominence in his community and even had access to the King (Ahab). His popularity and position no doubt indicates that his plate was full and his schedule was stacked. Until, he shared the long range weather forecast (three years with no rain) with the Royals.

I Kings 17:1 "As the Lord God of Israel lives, before whom I stand, there shall be no dew or rain these years, except by my word." For years I missed the *no dew* part. Things can get desperate in a hurry without this bit of morning moisture.

These words proved to be Elijah's farewell speech. After his sunny skies forecast, his popularity plummeted. The King was ready to kill him. Elijah was no doubt looking for an escape when the word of the Lord came to him saying, "Go and Hide at Cherith." (1 Kings 17:2). God had set up a place of protection for the prophet. Three years alone by a brook is a horrifying thought for the gregarious among us.

I wrapped up the Sunday school lesson that morning with the smug confidence that my insight and observations about Elijah would be meaningful to those in attendance. Perhaps that could even apply some points of the lesson to their everyday lives. After all, in verse one, Elijah is referred to as just the Tishbite and by the end of the chapter he is called the Man of God. The three years in the middle were a time of listening and learning.

Little did I realize that God was setting me up for my own little Cherith experience. No we didn't set up camp by a brook, but I now realize he set us aside for our protection. The next three years would be nothing like I had hope or dreamed. Despite my efforts to engage in my new location, it seemed that every opportunity dried up.

Neighbors, folks at church and even my husband's co-workers would smile sweetly and say things like, "let's get together." And despite our efforts, we never really made connections during our proverbial time by the brook. There were no invites to dinner... No backyard barbeques with friends. I felt like God had put me in time out!

There were many things God needed to teach me. He wanted me to settle down long enough to enjoy the magnificent man He had given me. He wanted me to delight in the extravagant gift of my two children. I now know that this place of seclusion was a place of His great protection and care. My life of distractions dissipated and in that quiet place I found the treasures of my lifetime... and time for my family and time to spend with God (after I got over being mad with Him for setting me aside).

My pleas for God to send the masses to befriend me and to end my lonely season were denied. God knew best. As a loving father he said, "No" to my childish requests for activities and parties with chocolate ice cream. He knew that the distractions I thrived on would be my downfall. His protection despite my protest was perfect.

He did allow me to meet one precious friend while I was there. I was standing in the church hallway, awkwardly going through the motions, trying desperately to fit in, when this girl approached me. She boldly asked, "Do you have any friends in Tennessee?" My quick response was, "No. Do you?" She laughed and responded, "No! I guess we should be friends!"

She was God's special gift to me during that dry season of my life. We laughed, we cried and kept each other from jumping off the bridge during a trying time in life. Even now (although a couple of states away) she is like a morning dew on the days I feel so parched.

Interestingly, after three years, our brook dried up (almost to the day) and God moved us back to our hometown. After this time of listening and learning, our perspective was different and our hearts were set on watering as many parched souls as God would send us.

Lesson Number Six: Good listeners are the best learners. In order to learn to use your time wisely, you have to block out the sounds of a hectic life and listen closely to God's instruction.

He said to them, "It is not for you to know the times or seasons that the Father has fixed by his own authority. But you will receive power when the Holy Spirit has come upon you, and you will be my witnesses in Jerusalem and in all Judea and Samaria, and to the end of the earth.

Acts 1:7–8 ESV

Watch Repair

"I have the spiritual gift of accessorizing," I heard a conference speaker say recently. The crowd of ladies roared with laughter and I quietly smiled (maybe a slight giggle) as I thought, "Oh, me too!" Now clearly my gift is not as extensive as hers. For heaven sake's, her readers matched her shoes! My accessory obsession is limited to watches. Yes, I have a watch fetish. At last count, I own twenty-nine of them. It obviously doesn't matter whether they keep time – as evidenced by the fact that I've worn several of them that didn't work for years.

So I find myself in a watch shop asking the watchmaker if my time pieces are broken. The reply comes as a relief. "No ma'am. Just no power." Those are powerful words.

How many times do we find ourselves dashing out the door with little time and no power?

A few Christmases ago I had my first revelation on the importance of power in our lives.

I have found that… whether you wait until the last minute or begin planning months ahead, it is difficult to come up with the perfect gift selection for Dads. I feel I always come up miserably short. A tie… a garden tool… it always seems impossible to come up with the right expression!

For years I thought my Daddy would be delighted with a pack of batteries. I guess it all started early with the standard Christmas stocking stuffer. We would all enjoy fun trinkets and candy in our stockings… but Santa always left Daddy a stocking full of batteries… D size, C size, Double As, Triple As. I just figured that it must have been something he requested. He always seemed to be pleased!

So soon, I jumped right in and over the years I have given him batteries and batteries accessories. One year I marveled at my stroke of genius to give him a rechargeable set.

I carried on this gift battery tradition to my husband. I guess it was then I realized what had been going on all these years! Despite my best intentions to bestow the perfect gift, I managed to pick something that had never been on their gift list. It was really kind of comical as I looked back. I felt pretty silly!

Those batteries had nothing To Do with (my perception of) his passion for a plenteous supply of power packs, battery gadgets and accessories... But it had everything To Do with us kids!

Amazingly, he was always equipped with batteries for my Chatty Cathy Doll, Double AAs for my son's game boy, Ds for the portable DVD player and C batteries for my daughter's Baby Alive. She would perform way too many bodily functions if her batteries were fresh!

Each holiday I have seen these guys unwrap the latest in battery technology and appear to be delighted... All these years these fellows have graciously received these gifts... unselfishly supplying the children with moments of fun and delight.

It reminds me of our vain attempts. We offer God the Father small packs of our own energy. I am sure, God, the source of all power and might is amused. But as a gracious Dad, he smiles waiting to give it back when we need it most.

Actually, our heavenly father is always giving the most precious gift of life (time and eternity). *For God so loved the world that he gave his only begotten son that whosoever believes in him should not perish but have everlasting life. John 3:16*

The Father gave; knowing our attempts to give back would be poor at best.

So this year the guy gift quandary is settled. The battery tradition may continue, but each year I add a resolve to give more time, love and attention to our heavenly Father.

Lesson Number Seven: By spending time with God in his word and in prayer we gain the necessary power to make it through a day filled with the deadlines and demands. Challenges will come but we can be confident knowing that we are fully charged.

"Then the Lord God took the man and put him into the Garden of Eden to cultivate it"

Genesis 2:15 NAS

Nine to Five

Work. It is a commandment. Exodus 20:9 spells it out very plainly. *Six days you shall labor and do all your work.* It is exampled by the Lord himself in Genesis Chapter two. In Genesis 2:15 it sounds heavenly. Cultivate it and keep it. I guess it was after the fall that work became a four letter word. Let's think about it. Gardening before there were weeds and thorns does in fact seem like paradise. The Lord created us to work and to create. How do we break that down? Eight hours a day? Does it come down to forty, sixty, eighty hours a week? How much of our work time should we devote to earning a wage? When is it time to clock out? These are all great time questions.

Let's carefully examine the work of God in those six days of creation. The text seems to equate work with creating. Maybe that's it! It is so satisfying to be creative or to produce a result. Work is an all encompassing term but often we consider work only what we get paid To Do. There is a good motive check in Proverbs 23:4. The scripture tells us <u>we should not</u> work to get rich.

Of course, we do many things that don't involve a paycheck. Creating a beautiful and clean living space for our family certainly falls in the work category and typically doesn't involve monetary gain. Intentionally teaching our children and caring for our loved ones is work. We can even throw in gardening, exercising and studying in the work category. Yes, work can even be fun, satisfying and enjoyable! God saw all he created and it was very good (Genesis 1:31.)

Remember the filter for time expenditures mentioned in chapter five? Is this activity getting me closer to my goal or is it increasing the distance between me and my goal? Let's tweak that in light of what God says about work in Proverbs 23:4. *Do not overwork to be rich; Because of your own understanding, cease!* That addresses quitting time. This scripture tells us that working to be *wealthy* is not an appropriate goal. If you have fallen for Satan's lie that the more you work, the more stuff you will have and the happier you will be, you need to reevaluate. If it is our intention to please God then we might want to think twice before we log in overtime. Besides, it is God that gives us increase!

Another time misnomer is the longer we work the more we get done! I think it is safe to assume the goal here is not to work longer and harder... exhausting ourselves, our bodies, our brains and our creativity but rather to focus on how to use the predetermined amount of time more efficiently.

Studies indicate that longer work hours DO NOT INCREASE productivity anyway! Many large companies are realizing this and in order to increase productivity they don't allow employees to work overtime. Research shows that most workers, even the most conscientious ones, were less productive and wasted more time if they anticipated overtime or just put in overtime, gratis. Working overtime may mean time-and-a-half pay at your company but even with proper compensation, it could also bring an increased risk of depression.

One study shows that people who work 11 or more hours a day have a more-than-doubled risk of a major depressive episode, compared with people who work the more-standard eight hours a day.

So when time runs out on Wednesday afternoon, you must have the discipline to draw the line on the list and say we will pick it up here tomorrow.

We often make the work effort way too complicated. It reminds me of an ambitious Wall Street tycoon who finally decided it was time to take a needed break. His travel agent booked a trip for him to the Marshall Islands. He was pleased with the accommodations and was amazed that no one had taken advantage of the money making potential of this exquisite South Pacific paradise. The dollar signs and possibilities were filling his head as he asked one of the locals where he could find a good fishing spot. The quick reply was "Henry's - a fishing pier on the west side of the island. He has a bait shop and some equipment to rent." So off to fish he went. When he arrived he found a poorly stocked, unattended hut. The longer he waited for assistance the more agitated he became with this poorly run, potential packed place. He looked down the long pier and could barely see a man sitting at the end… so he goes to ask the man where Henry might be. The man replied, "I am Henry. Can I help you?" The tycoon responded, "Can you help me? You need help! What a waste here! You have this heavenly paradise! You could make fortunes here, retire well, and do the things you have always wanted to do." Henry was a bit amused at the over exuberant entrepreneur. "You mean like fishing at the end of a long dock, on an island paradise, watching the sun set?" Henry said and smiled.

Yes, sometimes we make it way too complicated! I challenge you to resolve to make it simple. Prayerfully determine how much time you will devote to earning a wage. You are on the hook for six days to work and create.

Lesson Number Eight: Work shouldn't be about the wage. When we are working and creating we are reflecting the image of God.

Six days you shall do your work, and on the seventh day you shall rest, that your ox and your donkey may rest, and the son of your female servant and the stranger may be refreshed.

Exodus 23:12

Can I take a Nap?

Rest. God intends for us to have it. God set the example in creation itself. *"And on the seventh day God ended his work which he had made and rested on the seventh day from all his work and God blessed the seventh day and sanctified it." Gen 2:2.*

The benefits of getting the proper rest for our bodies are tremendous. Proper rest and relaxation affects us by replenishing our energy and mental alertness. It even plays a crucial role in metabolism (if I want to lose weight maybe I should take a nap)! Doctors prescribe rest to fight off sickness (even the common cold). We cannot ignore the resting component of our time management plan. As children we were given a bedtime. As adults we need to define where we fit in proper rest. We find a motivating reminder in 1 Corinthians 6:20, *"For you were bought at a (high) price; therefore glorify God in your body" NKJ*

I never considered scheduling daily rest. One day, a girlfriend of mine sensed that I was in dire need of a nap. I think my crankiness gave me away. She asked what my action plan for resting was, and truthfully, I was stumped. I thought we were talking about inaction, but the thought that I was going to have to plan my rest was overwhelming. Then I remembered God gave us the plan. This chapter points us to His plan and promise for us.

These are the roads I've traveled. Tired Trail. Overwhelmed Overpass. Frustrated Freeway. Exhausted Expressway. Perhaps you passed me on these overcrowded roadways. I traveled at such a high rate of speed that I would run right pass the exits that led to peaceful pastures and more restful roads. Trust me, this road race can easily end up in a crash!

I am always amazed at the relevance of God's word. It completely addresses our need for rest and rejuvenation.

It is easy to relate to the disciples in the second part of Mark 6:31. *"For there were many coming and going, and they did not even have time to eat."*

Ok, I've been there! At least, I didn't have time to eat properly. In this verse, Jesus cited the problem and told them what To Do about it. The problem was not enough time to take care of their own needs and the solution He gave them in the first part of the verse was clear.

And He said to them, "Come aside by yourselves to a deserted place and rest a while." An old friend of mine used to say, "You'd better come apart before you come apart."

I need to note something here. Before they made it to their place for resting, they were interrupted and called on to serve dinner for five thousand.

> *So they departed to a deserted place in the boat by themselves. But the multitudes saw them departing, and many knew Him and ran there on foot from all the cities. They arrived before them and came together to Him. And Jesus, when He came out, saw a great multitude and was moved with compassion for them, because they were like sheep not having a shepherd. So He began to teach them many things. When the day was now far spent, His disciples came to Him and said, "This is a deserted place, and*

> *already the hour is late. Send them away, that they*
> *may go into the surrounding country and villages*
> *and buy themselves bread; for they have nothing to*
> *eat." Mark 6:32-36 NKJ*

So don't be surprised as you head towards that place of rest, if you are called on to take care of a few thousand details before you get there! There was a time in my life that I couldn't even take a bath without someone banging on the bathroom door. Can you relate?

There comes a time, however, when you must send the crowd away and take the time to recharge.

> *Immediately He made His disciples get into the boat*
> *and go before Him to the other side, to Bethsaida,*
> *while He sent the multitude away. And when He*
> *had sent them away, He departed to the mountain*
> *to pray. Mark 6:45-46 NKJ*

This decision to dismiss the crowd may meet some resistance. It will require you to carefully guard your schedule. You will be required to set boundaries. This may be easier for some folks than others.

This is a tall order for me because I love the crowd! So I have to be determined to follow God's plan for rest. The temptation to hang around as long as the crowd is willing to stay can be detrimental (speaking from experience!).

Rest is important and God gave us a plan. *And on the seventh day God ended his work which he had made; and he rested on the seventh day from all his work which he had made.* Genesis 2:2 NKJ. A society without a Sabbath will soon become sick. We must draw the line and follow God's plan.

I love the prayer of Moses in Exodus 33 and the promise that God made to him in verse fourteen.

> *Now therefore, I pray, if I have found grace in Your sight, show me now Your way, that I may know You and that I may find grace in our sight. And consider that this nation is Your people." And He said, "My Presence will go with you, and I will give you rest."*

Our scheduling decisions must be made prayerfully asking the Lord to show us His way. Lesson Number Nine: In His Presence we will always find rest.

There is therefore now no condemnation to those who are in Christ Jesus, who do not walk according to the flesh, but according to the Spirit.

Romans 8:1 NKJ

THE CONDEMNATION
OF THE CLOCK

I have often glanced at the face of my watch, only to see (in my imagination) it displaying an expression of condemnation. A mad face displaying an angry look at my inability to get it all done, or a sad face, that time has passed without anything meaningful to show for it. But I long to see a glad face - when I am committed to allow the Lord *"to teach me to use wisely all the time I have." Psalms 90:12.*

In Chapter six, we discussed the importance of hearing the Holy Spirit and rejecting the noise of Satan, the accuser, who condemns and uses the clock in his arsenal of weapons. Readily accepting the Holy Spirit's nudging provides us comfort, while teaching us with God's eternal perspective.

Remember a To Do list packed with good deeds does not prove that we are good time mangers.

This two year study into the scripture, hammering out the principles of good time management has been eye opening! The things that I thought God mandated in the Bible for me to busy myself with aren't there! And many things that I thought were time wasters are exampled by the real people we find in the pages of scripture.

Real people. Living in reality. In the real world ... where the allotted time rarely meets our deadlines, demands or all the items on the daily To Do list.

I have a heritage of Godly women in my family. I grew up in a precious congregation where I had great examples of women who modeled many of the characteristics set forth in the 31st chapter of Proverbs. That Proverbs 31 woman is no stranger to us in the church world. But just as a quick review let's look at the list found in Proverbs 31 verses 10-31 NKJ.

Who can find a virtuous wife? For her worth is far above rubies.

The heart of her husband safely trusts her; so he will have no lack of gain.

She does him good and not evil all the days of her life. She seeks wool and flax, and willingly works with her hands.

She is like the merchant ships, she brings her food from afar. She also rises while it is yet night, and provides food for her household, and a portion for her maidservants.

She considers a field and buys it; from her profits she plants a vineyard. She girds herself with strength, and strengthens her arms.

She perceives that her merchandise is good, and her lamp does not go out by night. She stretches out her hands to the distaff,

and her hand holds the spindle. She extends her hand to the poor, yes, she reaches out her hands to the needy. She is not afraid of snow for her household, for all her household is clothed with scarlet. She makes tapestry for herself; her clothing is fine linen and purple.

Her husband is known in the gates, when he sits

among the elders of the land.

She makes linen garments and sells them,

and supplies sashes for the merchants.

Strength and honor are her clothing; she shall rejoice

in time to come.

She opens her mouth with wisdom, and on her

tongue is the law of kindness.

She watches over the ways of her household, and

does not eat the bread of idleness.

Her children rise up and call her blessed;

her husband also, and he praises her:

"Many daughters have done well,

but you excel them all."

Charm is deceitful and beauty is passing,

but a woman who fears the LORD, *she shall be*

praised.

Give her of the fruit of her hands,

and let her own works praise her in the gates.

Wow! That makes me tired! What a To Do list. The scripture doesn't mention this, but since it appears that she worked out (strengthens her arms), she was probably skinny too!

So for years I held this as the sacred outline for my To Do list! Talk about a time management nightmare. And *the accuser* was always quick to point out that I fell miserably short of this list. Maybe you've been there… trying to check off every good deed and task you can think of in an attempt to please… please people, even please God.

One day as I was researching Biblical time management principals, I had the most freeing revelation… the revelation of His Grace. It certainly isn't my long list of good things that will secure eternity for me.

Ephesians 2:8-9 For by Grace we are saved, not of works, lest any man should boast. Our impressive list won't cut it!

I knew that. As any good church girl I had that scripture memorized but perhaps my loose grip on grace (sometimes forgetting it is about His righteousness and not my goodness) resulted from Bible study that had been grab and go. Grab a Psalm. Throw in a Proverb. Glean a few feel good verses and I was on my way. But I had come to the point that I desperately needed an answer to my time dilemma, and I was sure that the answer could be found in God's blessed book.

Only God knows why I turned to the exhausting list in Proverbs. Verse one begins with the sayings of King Lemuel - An oracle that his Mother taught him. Moms with boys need to make sure they teach them this passage. Wait a minute! What? I thought this was God's To Do list for his girls! When in reality it is the sayings of King Lemuel as taught to him by his mother. Good grief! This is a mother-in-laws wish list for a daughter-in law!

I learned something that day. First of all, don't just pull out verse 10-31 and skip 1-9. It might change the whole perspective! And secondly, God wasn't looking for me to check off all the boxes on an unrealistic exhausting To Do list.

There are some other interesting observations about that chapter. In verse 3 she advises her son, "Don't give your strength to women." Let me break that down. In others words, there isn't anyone good enough for my son! In verse 10 she goes on to say, but Lemuel if you insist on finding a wife (doubt you will) these are the minimums you need to be looking for in my daughter-in-law.

Okay, so this woman who we have always praised for her poise and productivity is fictitious. **No doubt great things for us to aspire to!** A great dream girl list – a gal who would be praised by her husband, her children, her community and yes, even her mother-in-law.

In some ways I was disappointed because if I could have mastered the whole making the bed coverings thing and earned my real estate license, *me* and Proverbs 31 girl might have been neck-in–neck for the woman of the year. Not! I am just thankful that God doesn't condemn us if we don't have time to darn the socks in our household.

It did leave me with a hunger to find a real example in God's word of a woman who had it going on! So off I went looking for the real deal. A real woman, with a name, someone recorded in history, who despite the demands of life blessed the kingdom of God. I wanted to see a woman who led her family to God, was smart, was hospitable and understood the Grace of God. I needed to see a person in action who didn't have to become Polly Perfect by her own works.

I've noticed that there is a generation out there crying out for the real deal. They just want us (especially the church) to be authentic! Real! They are desperate to see examples of God working and transforming lives. The pretty, the polished and the perfect (fictitious) lives that some try to portray leaves the world hopeless with no way to measure up.

Instead, we need to strike that presentation and serve up God's Grace with a side of authenticity. God's work instead of our work. God's Excellence. That will always be the real picture of Beauty!

Such is the case in Acts Chapter 16. We find a real girl with a real name. Lydia. Lydia was Greek even though she lived in a Roman settlement.

She was a well-to-do agent of purple-dye. She was a business woman. We find her insisting on extending hospitality to Paul and his companions who were on a journey traveling through the region of Philippi.

The text mentions members of her household being baptized and several scholars speculate that she was a single parent.

Scripture tells us that she was a God fearing Gentile. She is considered to be "the first 'European' Christian convert". Let's read her story. It is short, sweet and to the point.

> *Acts 16:13-16 (NKJV) And on the Sabbath day we went out of the city to the riverside, where prayer was customarily made; and we sat down and spoke to the women who met there. Now a certain woman named Lydia heard us. She was a seller of purple from the city of Thyatira, who worshiped God. The Lord opened her heart to heed the things spoken by Paul. And when she and her household were baptized, she begged us, saying, "If you have judged me to be faithful to the Lord, come to my house and stay." So she persuaded us.*

Lydia listened for God's word. She was a worshipper. She opened her heart. This woman is the real deal!

At the end of the day (or at least the end of the chapter) the Proverbs 31 woman receives the reward that we often strive for - praise from her husband... praise from her children... praise from her community.

But the real deal Lydia (a hardworking gal who no doubt had a full schedule) gave her time to advance the kingdom of God. The work of God was accomplished and as a worshipper she gave her praise to God!

And for the world looking for the real deal… let's live like Lydia.

Lesson Number Ten: A good companion for a full schedule is a heart full of worship.

But those who wait on the L*ORD* *shall renew their strength; They shall mount up with wings like eagles, They shall run and not be weary, They shall walk and not faint.*

Isaiah 40:31 NKJ

WORTH THE WAIT!

There are not many hands that go up when you ask the question, "Who wants to play the waiting game?" Yes, it does matter how you play the game. Let's explore the rules of waiting to win.

Rule #1: When you are waiting on God, you must realize the prize is always worth the wait. The Bible contains so many examples of people in waiting mode. If you are waiting for something in your life, you are in good company. We find many of the Faith's Hall of Fame sitting patiently (some not so patiently) at the stop lights of life. Some are waiting or hoping for a better future. Others are waiting for God's promise to be fulfilled or for their dreams to become reality.

Rule #2: Stay on track. Noah is a great example of staying busy, being productive and staying on track during the 120 year wait. His unwavering commitment to complete the task God gave him is inspiring. No doubt folks in his neighborhood constantly criticized his bazaar behavior. Building a boat without a lake or a raindrop in sight must have seemed a bit crazy. Noah can go on the waiting game winners' board because he scored by saving his family and two of every living creature. We should also note that he waited well. In Exodus 7 we find that God rewarded Noah for a job well done.

> *Then God spoke to Noah and to his sons with him, saying: "And as for Me, behold, I establish My covenant with you and with your descendants after you. Genesis 9:8-9 NKJ*

Job, known for his patience, also goes on the leader board. Job had no certain task to complete during his wait. I think this might be more difficult. Have you noticed that time seems to go faster if you are busy? Disaster management was the only thing to fill Job's time as he waited for the storms of life to pass. Job declared his confidence in God as he waited. He is a winner!

> *Now the LORD blessed the latter days of Job more than his beginning. Job 42:12 NKJ*

Joseph (mentioned in chapter three and in the book of Genesis) mastered rule number three. **Rule #3: No whining while you wait.** Resisting the temptation to whine, complain, or protest is essential to winning. Maybe you have been sold out, overlooked, lied about and forgotten as you waited for that promised promotion. Joseph could certainly relate.

We should take a few pages out of Joseph's play book. We need to put our hand to the task of making our surroundings better while we wait. Decorating the prison cell is great practice for adorning the palace.

> *And his master saw that the LORD was with him (Joseph) and that the LORD made all he did to prosper in his hand. - Genesis 39:3 NKJ.*

Remember this took place as he waited. Waiting is a popular theme in scripture, but I think the waiting story of

Abraham and Sarah is one of the most interesting. Their story illustrates that wavering during waiting can produce the worst of situations. We can call this a wait warning. We can learn from our own mistakes, but it makes more sense to learn from the mistakes of others! First Lady Eleanor Roosevelt, the wife of the Franklin D. Roosevelt, once said — "Learn from the mistakes of others. You can't live long enough to make them all yourself." Amen, Sista!

The story begins in Genesis 15 as God makes a promise to Abraham that his offspring would be too numerous to count.

The promise was made. You are going to have a child and become a mighty nation. This is the beginning of a long wait. Even if Abraham and Sarah had been newlyweds when the promise was made, they would have been decorating the nursery after their silver wedding anniversary. That would have been strange enough, but this promise was made when Abraham was seventy-five years old. The proud parents didn't have their precious promise until he was one hundred.

Do you wait well? For those of us with short attention spans, waiting can get hairy. It takes commitment to stay on track and confidence that the promise will be delivered in due time.

Lest we think that God makes promises and gives no thought to when they will be delivered, let's look at Genesis 18:14. In verse 14, God says that the promise will be delivered at the appointed time. Some translations put it this way - at the set time. When God made the promise he set the time! We need to learn to trust God to set the time and keep the time. God's timing, not ours, is always perfect.

A couple of months with no sign of the promise is one thing. But when the years and decades drag on we must make a decision not to let discouragement set in. God's promises are sure.

The promise of a child at 75 (Genesis 15) seemed a bit farfetched. As time rolled on, Sarah lost faith in this implausible promise. This is the danger zone. When you are tired of waiting don't be tempted to take matters into your own hands.

Now Sarah, Abram's wife, had borne him no children. And she had an Egyptian maidservant whose name was Hagar. ² So Sarah said to Abram, "See now, the LORD has restrained me from bearing children. Please, go in to my maid; perhaps I shall obtain children by her." And Abram heeded the voice of Sarah. ³ Then Sarah, Abram's wife, took Hagar her maid, the Egyptian, and gave her to her husband Abram to be his wife, after Abram had dwelt ten years in the land of Canaan. ⁴ So he went in to Hagar, and she conceived. And when she saw that she had conceived, her mistress became despised in her eyes. Genesis 16:1-4 NJK

The consequences of her bright idea were colossal! Thousands of years later we are still feeling the effects of Sarah's attempt to help God. This act of impatience was the birth of a conflict that continues today in the Middle East.

One of the most important rules of the waiting game is **Rule #4: Shortcuts can result in a huge penalty.** You can't go straight from second base to home plate. You will be called out for that inning and the final score will be affected. Have you ever tried to save time and instead made a massive mess?

In chapter 21 of Genesis (verse one) we see that the Lord was gracious to Sarah and did what He promised. God's plan prevails despite our destructive decisions. Abraham and Sarah were finally able to celebrate the joy, laughter and the promise of a great and mighty nation.

Rule #5 for the waiting game: It is okay to revel in winning as long as you realize you are not responsible for victory. A declaration that God always keeps His promises is appropriate. Showing gratitude that our sins can't thwart His plan is fitting. I challenge you to show your best sportsmanship while you are waiting to win!

Lesson Number Eleven: God's promises are worth the wait!

Watch therefore, for you do not know when the master of the house is coming—in the evening, at midnight, at the crowing of the rooster, or in the morning...

Mark 13:25

WHEN THE CLOCK STRIKES MIDNIGHT

Cinderella is the expert here. She ran out of time, became dazzled by the allure of the night and simply lost track of time. We have more at stake than this fairy tale princess, and it is important for us to keep our eye on the clock. Scripture tells us how to prepare and be watchful. Let's see how to keep our carriage from turning into a pumpkin.

We all face deadlines every day. A deadline indicates that there is a time limit. We are given a timeframe to get it all done. This is our dilemma! Do we do the dishes or dance the night away? If Cinderella had stayed home doing her chores she would have never connected with the Prince. The reality here is that although we must take care of the daily dirty dishes, we need to schedule some dancing along the way!

We must remember that we need to strike the perfect balance. If you spend all day every day washing dishes, you have too many dishes! Less dishes means more time for dancing!

Part of our time dilemma stems from the much-ness of our lives. Cinderella only had one dress option. That was certainly a time saver! Last Sunday I tried on eight outfits and was 10 minutes late to church thanks to my much-ness!

Inventorying our lives is a great place to start in our effort to manage our time effectively. By giving serious thought to the way we spend time and contemplating the eternal effects of our actions, we can be on our way to realizing our happily ever after (eternity with Christ)!

Several years of my life were spent in a newsroom. I knew that at 6 o'clock sharp the red tally light would come on and, ready or not, I was "live" for the next 30 minutes. Each day I prepared and paced myself. Frankly, it was very manageable because I knew when to expect the deadline. Cinderella was also given the luxury of a curfew. She knew when time would run out. It certainly would have made things easier if she would have taken the time to exchange phone numbers with the Prince early in the evening.

Our ultimate deadline is uncertain. No doubt the *times up* moment will arrive but we don't know when.

When will our time run out? Since no one knows the day or the hour, we should make sure that all of our time is used wisely and we are prepared for life after death. We need to make sure that we consider - the ultimate goal is not just today's deadline. Let's make sure we are mindful of the eternal effects of how we invest our time.

I used to think I would like to know how much time I had on this earth. What was I thinking? With my tendency to procrastinate, that would be a disaster! I can see a lifetime of purpose put off until the last half hour!

The *dead line* – I never saw it that way before! We don't like to think about our own mortality. This life is like a vapor the scripture tells us. In comparison to eternity, the few fleeing years we have here pale in comparison to time in eternity. Our focus to manage our time at this dance needs to take into consideration what happens after midnight.

We need to keep our eye on the clock. Wasting time with meaningless activity when you could be on the dance floor with the Prince, is not wise. Our primary reason for being at the dance is to make a connection with the Prince. That is the whole point!

Lesson Number Twelve: A connection made with the *Prince of Peace* beats out glass slippers and a pretty dress every time. Remember we are going for the *happily ever after* (John 3:16)!

Therefore if the Son makes you free, you shall be free indeed.

John 8:36 NKJ

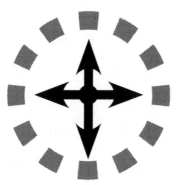

THE CROSS CANCELS THE CURSE OF THE CLOCK

I am from the sunny South. It is a picturesque place with moss draped oak trees. It is a coastal community that is hopping with fun beaches and lots of history. Our beautiful springs, lovely late falls and mild winters make it the perfect tourist spot. There is really only one negative thing. Our summers are HOT and Humid. Our Spas don't need Saunas.

Despite your best efforts to straighten your natural curly hair, 43 seconds after stepping outside it'll curl and stick flat to your head. I don't mean to make anybody blush, but my Grandmother put it best. One day we were running errands and got into the hot car... the AC hadn't caught up yet... and she said to me. "Good Grief! It is hotter than a June Bride in a feather bed in here!" Imagine my shock... "well, Grandmother!" But frankly that was the best description ever!

I had some friends visiting and they wanted a tour of our historic district. So off I went to play tour guide. I took them to the high spots which included some of our cemeteries... not the lively part of the tour but interesting none-the-less. Button Gwinnett, one of the Signers of the Declaration of Independence, is buried in our colonial cemetery. The composer of the Christmas classic Jingle Bells, James Pierpoint, is also interred in our town. He served as a music director in one of our churches in the 1800s.

I was amused as I looked at his tombstone on that hot, blistery Savannah day. "Dashing through the snow?" How did he come up with that? Dashing through the pollen maybe? Through the Steam? Through the Humidity? But the Snow?

The only dashing I'd seen were folks dashing from place to place, from commitment to commitment, from appointment to appointment. I observed that dashing takes its toll. Dashing is designed for a short sprint. Dashing is not for an endurance race. And I found myself in the fast lane of life, wanting to add another verse to that song... Dashing through the day I've got those bills to pay!

One morning I woke up, looked in the mirror and I saw a frantic, tired, overwhelmed church girl. Oh, I had all the boxes on my To Do list checked off, my packed schedule and polished presentation might have fooled some people, but I knew my soul was starving. Out of desperation, I turned to the scriptures I had learned as a kid in Sunday school.

God was gracious again that morning and reminded me of the words written in red in Matthew 11:28. *"Come unto me all who are weary and heavy laden and I will give you rest."* That was it! I needed rest for my soul. It was falling apart and being squeezed to death by a grueling schedule. That day my time management plan changed dramatically. I had trusted Christ for grace to cover my soul as a child and that day I trusted him with the grace to cover my schedule.

A few months later I signed up for a course at the local synagogue. They were offering a class on Jewish traditions and customs and I thought that would be interesting. This would be a reminder to me on the time management issue.

The rabbi opened the second session with the Institution of the Jewish calendar. "We are in Year 5775", he said.

The Rabbi explained that the Hebrew calendar was first established when the people of God were freed from Egyptian bondage. This first tool of time keeping signified their freedom from slavery.

You see, slaves have no mastery of their own time. Time really began for God's chosen when they were redeemed from that Egyptian Bondage. For centuries they had been bound by a task master.

Likewise, the Cross of Christ cancels the curse of sin and redeems us from its bondage. The chains of time and this fleeting life no longer bind us. The Cross of Christ offers us eternal life and sets us on course to the promise land. My sweet friends, the promise land is a place where time will be no more!

TIME CAPSULES

These can be taken several times a day. Unlimited refills. Proven to be a great stress reliever!

__Ephesians 5:15-17__ Look carefully then how you walk, not as unwise but as wise, making the best use of the time, because the days are evil. Therefore do not be foolish, but understand what the will of the Lord is.

__Psalm 90:12__ So teach us to number our days that we may get a heart of wisdom.

__Ecclesiastes 3:8__ A time to love, and a time to hate; a time for war, and a time for peace.

__Matthew 6:33__ But seek first the kingdom of God and his righteousness, and all these things will be added to you.

Colossians 4:5 *Walk in wisdom toward outsiders, making the best use of the time.*

Psalm 39:4-5 *O Lord, make me know my end and what is the measure of my days; let me know how fleeting I am! Behold, you have made my days a few handbreadths, and my lifetime is as nothing before you. Surely all mankind stands as a mere breath! Selah*

James 4:13-17 *Come now, you who say, "Today or tomorrow we will go into such and such a town and spend a year there and trade and make a profit"— yet you do not know what tomorrow will bring. What is your life? For you are a mist that appears for a little time and then vanishes. Instead you ought to say, "If the Lord wills, we will live and do this or that." As it is, you boast in your arrogance. All such boasting is evil. So whoever knows the right thing To Do and fails To Do it, for him it is sin.*

2 Peter 3:8-14 *But do not overlook this one fact, beloved, that with the Lord one day is as a thousand years, and a thousand years as one day. The Lord is not slow to fulfill his promise as some count slowness, but is patient toward you, not wishing that any should perish, but that all should reach repentance.*

Matthew 24:36 *But concerning that day and hour no one knows, not even the angels of heaven, nor the Son, but the Father only.*

Psalm 31:14-15 *But I trust in you, O Lord; I say, "You are my God." My times are in your hand; rescue me from the hand of my enemies and from my persecutors!*

Acts 1:7-8 *He said to them, "It is not for you to know times or seasons that the Father has fixed by his own authority. But you will receive power when the Holy Spirit has come upon you, and you will be my witnesses in Jerusalem and in all Judea and Samaria, and to the end of the earth."*

Galatians 4:4 *But when the fullness of time had come, God sent forth his Son, born of woman, born under the law*

John 9:4 *We must work the works of him who sent me while it is day; night is coming, when no one can work.*

Proverbs 3:1-2 *My son, do not forget my teaching, but let your heart keep my commandments, for length of days and years of life and peace they will add to you.*

Acts 17:31 *Because he has fixed a day on which he will judge the world in righteousness by a man whom he has appointed; and of this he has given assurance to all by raising him from the dead."*

James 1:5 *If any of you lacks wisdom, let him ask God, who gives generously to all without reproach, and it will be given him.*

Jeremiah 1:5 *Before I formed you in the womb I knew you, and before you were born I consecrated you; I appointed you a prophet to the nations.*

Isaiah 60:22 *The least one shall become a clan, and the smallest one a mighty nation; I am the Lord; in its time I will hasten it.*

John 3:16-17 *For God so loved the world, that he gave his only Son, that whoever believes in him should not perish but have eternal life. For God did not send his Son into the world to condemn the world, but in order that the world might be saved through him.*

Esther 4:14 *For if you keep silent at this time, relief and deliverance will rise for the Jews from another place, but you and your father's house will perish. And who knows whether you have not come to the kingdom for such a time as this?*

Psalm 139:7 *Where can I go from your Spirit? All the days ordained for me were written in your book before one of them came to be.*

1 Timothy 4:14-16 *Do not neglect your gift, which was given you through a prophetic message when the body of elders laid their hands on you. Be diligent in these matters; give yourself wholly to them, so that everyone may see your progress. Watch your life and doctrine closely. Persevere in them, because if you do, you will save both yourself and your hearers.*

Hebrews 6:11-12 *We want each of you to show this same diligence to the very end, in order to make your hope sure. We do not want you to become lazy, but to imitate those who through faith and patience inherit what has been promised.*

Proverbs 19:21 *Many are the plans in a man's heart, but it is the Lord's purpose that prevails.*

Deuteronomy 4:29 *But if from there you seek the LORD your God, you will find him if you look for him with all your heart and with all your soul.*

Proverbs 21:5 *The plans of the diligent lead to profit as surely as haste leads to poverty.*

2 Timothy 1:9 *This grace was given us in Christ Jesus before the beginning of time*

John 3:16 *For God so loved the world that He gave His only begotten Son, that whoever believes in Him should not perish but have everlasting life.*

Time Quotes

'If you judge people, you have no *time* to love them." - Mother Teresa

"Time is an illusion." - Albert Einstein

"You may delay, but time will not." -Benjamin Franklin

"How did it get so late so soon? It's night before it's afternoon. December is here before it's June. My goodness how the time has flewn. How did it get so late so soon?" - Dr.Suess

"The future is something which everyone reaches at the rate of sixty minutes an hour, whatever he does, whoever he is." -C.S. Lewis

"The future starts today, not tomorrow." -John Paul II

"In the West we have a tendency to be profit-oriented, where everything is measured according to the results and we get caught up in being more and more active to generate results. In the East -- especially in India -- I find that people are more content to just be, to just sit around under a banyan tree for half a day chatting to each other. We Westerners would probably call that wasting time. But there is value to it. Being with someone, listening without a clock and without anticipation of results, teaches us about love. The success of love is in the loving -- it is not in the result of loving. " - Mother Teresa, *A Simple Path: Mother Teresa*

"Time is too slow for those who wait, too swift for those who fear, too long for those who grieve, too short for those who rejoice, but for those who love, time is eternity." - Henry van Dyke

ACKNOWLEDGEMENTS

*Thanks to **all** those who listened to my dreams, supported me, read drafts or wondered how God could ever use a mess like me to convey a message like this. God heard your prayers.*

Thanks for the encouragement extended by Bucky Burnsed, Kyle Burnsed, Kari Burnsed, Jerry and Ken Walters (the world's best parents), Debbie VanCott, Cathy Rodgers, Belinda Baptiste, Renee Moore, Emra Smith, Sarah and Ronnie Williams, Stacy Bettis, Sally Watson, Trina Bowen, Sarah Westcott, Larry McDaniel, Laura Fulford, Kenny and Shirley Grant, Eddie and O.J Dennis, Danny and Carol Falligant, Jim and Barbara Rush, Billy and Sonja Miller, Jim Smith and Louise Smith (who now really understands time), Glynda Smith, Lisa Yanette, Catherine Smith, Brooke Chambers, Joan White, Linda Znachko, Janee White, Beth Delnostro, Ena Hunphries, Kim Albright, Debbie Nash, Kelly Applegate, Karen and Barry Moore, Jean and Bubba Cribb, Brenda and Chris Sather, Doris and Brinson Clements, Rabbi Ruven Barkan, Tina Browning and Mary Lawrence Kennickell.

Special thanks to Christine Loughman at Westbow Press and to Karen Pearson (who God sent at the perfect time).

ABOUT THE AUTHOR

Kathy was sitting in the lobby of the radio station where I worked. She was waiting to be interviewed for the Program Director's job for the new Christian station that would sign on soon. It was our first meeting. I didn't make a good impression but that's for another time (intentional pun). Despite the poor start, a short time later we began dating and were married in two years' time.

If you think keeping time in a radio station is important then you are right. The hour is counted to the minute and the second. Later, our careers took both of us into TV where again time is counted to the minute and the second.

It would be very easy to assume Kathy knows what time it is. More times than not she doesn't. The curse of the clock has never stressed my wife. On TV she relied on a Floor Director to count her down. When it counted she could make it work right down to the second. The rest of her life is not like that. For her, time is nothing more than a constantly persistent irritant.

Kathy is a classic psychological study in what's not apparent. When meeting her, it would be easy to assume she is a Polly Anna. She's not. Or simple. She's not. Or shallow. She's not. Or incapable of the big project. Definitely not.

All of her life she has functioned above expectations. She was 19 when she applied for and got the Program Director's job at the radio station. A year later she was anchoring the news on the local ABC-TV affiliate. She directed the Media Ministries at our church to include hosting more than 1500 half-hour programs all-the-while successfully birthing our two children.

Unlike men, like me, who if you tell them not to do something they will probably do it, Kathy is different. If you tell her she can't do something she'll prove you wrong, just like when our church was doing a live nativity and the pastor said to her, "You can't find a camel." She found two, provided free and the men who cared for them. So when this book idea came along she needed little pushing. I simply said, "You? You're going to write a book? Sure." After 31 years of marriage we have learned how to push each other's buttons.

When you think about it though it makes perfect sense for Kathy to write about Time Management. After all, who would want to read a book written by someone who was born as the perfect time manager? I, for one, would be skeptical of their integrity. Rather, Kathy speaks very candidly from her own point of view about time and its effect on us, the human race. More importantly, she shares God's point of view on time. After 33 years I can tell you this; what you've read is true. It's honest. It's sometimes unvarnished and it comes from her own walk with God, the only real master of space and time. This book was a treat! ~Bucky Burnsed

For more information about

Kathy Walters Burnsed

please visit:

www.PerfectTimingToday.com

kathy@PerfectTimingToday.com

PerfectTimingToday@gmail.com

www.facebook.com/PerfectTimingToday

Invite Kathy to Speak. She combines inspiration, motivation and humor to delight audiences large and small.

Kathy's variety of presentation options and her ability to connect and bring encouragement could be the perfect fit for your next meeting or event. Your team, church, business or organization could reap positive benefits from time with Kathy.

Available to speak to, train, energize and inspire your members, volunteers or employees.